Stage 1+
Songbirds Phonics

**Clare Kirtley
and Thelma Page**

Teaching Notes

Contents

Top Cat

Sam's Pot

Bob Bug

Dig, Dig, Dig!

Zak and the Vet

Mum Bug's Bag

Introduction

These books present highly decodable texts that children can read by sounding out and blending. They provide a reading context through which children can discover and understand that there is a code to reading. The explicit usefulness of phonics is emphasised in a variety of exciting reading books, all by popular, award-winning children's author, Julia Donaldson.

The focus phonics are listed on the cover of each book. By introducing these and the skills of sounding out and blending prior to reading, the children will be equipped with the necessary knowledge to confidently and successfully read unfamiliar words in the books. The books consolidate letter-sound knowledge and practise the skills of sounding out and blending, reinforcing decoding as a reading strategy that children can use to become fluent, independent and capable readers. These notes describe activities to learn the focus phonics prior, during and after group or independent reading. The amount of time spent introducing the phonics prior to reading will of course depend on the ability of the children. They also include ideas for developing children's language comprehension. These ideas include suggestions for teaching the skills of prediction, questioning, clarifying, summarising and imagining in order to help children understand the text and the whole stories.

The inclusion of words that do not use the focus phonics being introduced or studied previously has been kept to a minimum while keeping the texts meaningful. Such words, often high frequency words, can be introduced and compared with the decodable words before studying the texts. The children can be encouraged to read such words in the text using several reading strategies such as sounding out, rereading to check it makes sense, context and sight vocabulary. Therefore such words are listed as 'Context' words.

These books provide the ideal resource for children to decode, understand and reflect on what has been written, responding to the varied ideas, themes and events and thus engaging in reading for pleasure. They fully support a synthetic approach to teaching reading and follow the introduction of grapheme-phoneme correspondences outlined in *Playing with Sounds*.

Glossary

Phoneme – a sound in a word (e.g. *cat, shop, sky, light* and *rain* all have three phonemes or three separate sounds)

Grapheme – a letter or sequence of letters that represents a phoneme (e.g in *rain* each of the three phonemes is represented by a grapheme *r – ai – n*; in *light* each of the three phonemes is represented by a grapheme, namely *l – igh – t).*

Context words – words which do not use the focus phonics but which are needed for the story.

Top Cat

Focus phonics	Skills, concepts and knowledge covered by the Teaching Notes	Example phonic words	PNS Literacy Framework
The sound made by: m c t p a o	**Skills** – Blend two or three sounds together to make words; Segment simple CVC words into their individual sounds **Concepts** – Words consist of sounds; Sounds in words are represented by letters **Knowledge** – Focus phonics	**Example phonic words** am top cat pop **Context words** I **Letters and sounds** Phase 2 A sound in a word can be represented by one letter or more than one letter (sets 1–5)	YF **W** 5.2, 5.5, 5.9 **C** 7.1

Sam's Pot

Focus phonics	Skills, concepts and knowledge covered by the Teaching Notes	Example phonic words	PNS Literacy Framework
The sound made by: s m c t g p a o	**Skills** – Blend three sounds together to make words; Segment simple CVC into their individual sounds **Concepts** – Words consist of sounds; Sounds in words are represented by letters **Knowledge** – Focus phonics	**Example phonic words** Tom got pot Pam Sam pat tap mop cat **Context words** a **Letters and sounds** Phase 2 A sound in a word can be represented by one letter or more than one letter (sets 1–5)	YF **W** 5.2, 5.5, 5.9 **C** 7.1

Key

C = Language comprehension   Y = Year

W = Word recognition   F = Foundation/reception

In the designations such as 5.2, the first number represents the strand and the second number the individual objective

Bob Bug

Focus phonics	Skills, concepts and knowledge covered by the Teaching Notes	Example phonic words
The sound made by: r l d b f h i u s m c t g p a o	**Skills** – Blend two or three sounds together to make words; Segment simple CVC words into their individual sounds **Concepts** – Words consist of sounds; Sounds in words are represented by letters **Knowledge** – Focus phonics	Bob is bug has mum His big dad fit cup It lid cot rug bad rat hug sip **Context words** a **Letters and sounds** Phase 2 A sound in a word can be represented by one letter or more than one letter (sets 1–5) **PNS Literacy Framework** YF (W) 5.2, 5.5, 5.9 (C) 7.3

Dig, Dig, Dig!

Focus phonics	Skills, concepts and knowledge covered by the Teaching Notes	Example phonic words
The sound made by: r l d b f h i u s m t g p a o n	**Skills** – Blend two, three or four sounds together to make words; Segment simple CVC words into their individual sounds **Concepts** – Words consist of sounds; Sounds in words are represented by letters **Knowledge** – Focus phonics	dig Tim and his dog had fun dug up lot mud rag bus lid big tin in it lots bugs **Context words** a of **Letters and sounds** Phase 2 A sound in a word can be represented by one letter or more than one letter (sets 1–5) **PNS Literacy Framework** YF (W) 5.2, 5.5, 5.8 (C) 7.3

Zak and the Vet

Focus phonics	Skills, concepts and knowledge covered by the Teaching Notes	Example phonic words	PNS Literacy Framework
The sound made by: v w y z j n k e r d b f h i u s m c	**Skills** – Blend three or four sounds together to make words; Segment simple CVC words into their individual sounds **Concepts** – Words consist of sounds; Sounds in words are represented by letters; There can be more than one way to represent a sound **Knowledge** – Focus phonics	sit Zak did not ran and in fog red van hit him Jen went vet had bad cut get jab yes wag **Context words** a better He the to will **Letters and sounds** Phase 2 A sound in a word can be represented by one letter or more than one letter (sets 1–5)	YF **W** 5.2, 5.5, 5.9 **C** 7.3

Mum's Bug Bag

Focus phonics	Skills, concepts and knowledge covered by the Teaching Notes	Example phonic words	PNS Literacy Framework
The sound made by: w y z j n k e r d b f h i u s m c t g p a o	**Skills** – Blend three sounds together to make words; Segment simple CVC words into their individual sounds **Concepts** – Words consist of sounds; Sounds in words are represented by letters; There can be more than one way to represent a sound **Knowledge** – Focus phonics	Mum Bug has red bag zip can fit pen in and fan bun pot jam get wet yuk gets big **Context words** a her hole of the **Letters and sounds** Phase 2 A sound in a word can be represented by one letter or more than one letter (sets 1–5)	YF **W** 5.2, 5.5, 5.8 5.9 **C** 7.3

Top Cat

Focus phonics				
m	am mat	*p*	top pop
c	cat	*a*	am cat mat
t	top cat mat	*o*	top pop

C = Language comprehension   R, *AF* = QCA reading assessment focus

W = Word recognition   W, *AF* = QCA writing assessment focus

Introducing the phonics

W *Initial sounds display*
Make a display of objects which begin with each of the focus sounds (e.g. *mat, cup, teddy, pan, apple, orange*). Encourage children to draw pictures of objects, or make models out of construction kits, to add to the display. Give the children different pens, pencils and chalks to practise writing the letters.

W *Letter formation*
Make letter cards by writing the focus letters on individual pieces of card. Stress the correct letter formation as you do so and encourage the children to sky-write the letters.

W *Quick sounds*
Ask the children to say the sound usually made by each letter as you point to it. Vary the order.

W *Blending sounds*
Draw three boxes in a row, as a phoneme frame, on a board. Display the letter cards (or magnetic letters) around it. Pick three cards and place them, one in each box, to make a word (*cat, mat, pat, top, pop, mop, cop, cot, pot*). Tell the children that each of these letters makes one sound in a word. Ask the children to say the sound of each letter as you point to it. Then tell the children that you are going to blend the letters together to make the word. Say the sounds altogether and ask the children to say them with you to read the word.

Group or guided reading

Before reading

(**C**) *(Clarifying)* Ask the children to find the title of the story. Explain that the *top* person can mean the most important person in a group and that the *top* of something is also the highest part of something. For example, the *top* of a mountain is the highest point.

(**W**) Ask the children to look at the letters in the box on the back cover of their books and tell you the sound usually made by each letter in words. Can the children think of any words that begin with each of these letters? (They can look at your display if you have one.) Tell the children that most of the words in this book use these letters so they can sound out each letter and blend them together to read the words, just as you did together when reading the words you wrote in the phoneme frame.

(**C**) *(Questioning)* Ask the children to find and point to the first word on the first page.

Strategy check

Read the first word *I* and explain that this is a word they will meet a lot in stories and the children should look out for it in this story. Ask the children to point at the text, moving along the line from left to right.

Independent reading

(**W**) Encourage each of the children to read the whole book at his or her own pace, pointing at the words, sounding out and blending words they do not recognise and remembering to look out for the word *I*. Listen in to each child reading and provide lots of praise and support.

● Praise the children if they can match one spoken word to one written word.

● Praise them for sounding out and blending sounds to read words.

Assessment Observe the children to check that they can:

▪ *(R, AF1)* point at the text, moving along the line from left to right

▪ *(R, AF1)* confidently give the sound for all the focus letters

▪ *(R, AF1)* successfully blend the two sounds for *am* together and recognise it as the word *am*

▪ *(R, AF1)* successfully blend the three sounds for *top* together and recognise it as the word *top*

▪ *(R, AF1)* recognise repeated words

- (R, AF1) notice the change in word order on pages 2 and 4.

Emphasise and model these skills for any child who needs help.

Returning to the text

Ask the children to:

Ⓦ Find a word in the text beginning with the sound *c*, sound out all the letters in the word and then blend them together to read the word. Repeat for words beginning with *a* then *t*.

Ⓦ Find the picture of the cat sitting on the mat. Think of other words which rhyme with *cat* (e.g. *chat, bat, hat, pat, rat*).

Ⓦ Shut the book and segment *cat* into its separate sounds, ready for writing. Have a go at writing *cat* on a board. Blend the sounds together again. Find it in the book to check.

Ⓦ *Change one letter*
Change one letter of *cat* to write *pat*, then *mat* and *map*.

Assessment Observe the children to check that they can:

- (R, AF1) remember the letter that makes the sound *c*, the sound *a* and the sound *t*

- (R, AF1) generate words which rhyme with *cat.*

Model the appropriate responses for children who need help. Follow this up with further practice using the Blending Activity, Letter Pattern Activity and Segmenting Activity for *Top Cat* on the *eSongbirds* CD-ROM, as well as additional practice reading *Top Cat* using the Talking Story version.

Where next?

Further phonic practice

Ⓦ Ask the children to write *top* on a board. Think of other words that rhyme with *top* (*mop, cop*) and segment the new words into their separate sounds, saying each sound in isolation as you write it. Then blend the sounds together while pointing at each sound.

Extension phonic work

Ⓒ *(Imagining)* Ask the children to write and illustrate a *Top* story using the ideas and same structure as the story, e.g. *I am top boy/girl.*

Sam's Pot

Focus phonics				
s	Sam	g	got
m	Sam Pam mop	p	pot pat mop
c	cat	a	Sam Pam pat
t	Tom got pot pat	o	got pot mop

C = Language comprehension   *R, AF* = QCA reading assessment focus

W = Word recognition   *W, AF* = QCA writing assessment focus

Introducing the phonics

W Read familiar rhyming poems and stories. Stop before the rhyming word and get the children to supply it.

W *Spot the rhymes*
Display pictures (or objects) of rhyming things (*cat, mat, bat, pot, cot, dot, mop, top, shop, map, cap, tap, dog, log, mug, rug, bug*). Ask the children to come up and find two things that rhyme. Pick two pictures that share only the same end sound (*cat/pot*). Say the words, stressing the end sound and ask the children what sound they can hear at the end of these words.

W *Robot talk*
Use a puppet or a robot made out of junk materials to say words in a special robotic way. Tell the children the robot says all the sounds in words separately and they have to blend the sounds together to tell you what the robot is saying. Make the robot say one of the words for the rhyming pictures (e.g. *c – a – t*), and tell the children to look at the pictures to help them.

Group or guided reading

Before reading

C *(Prediction)* Ask the children to say what they think might be in Sam's pot in the picture on the front cover.

Ⓦ Ask the children to look at the letters in the box on the back cover of their books and tell you the sound usually made by each letter in words. Can the children think of any words that begin or end with any of these letters?

Ⓦ Tell the children that the words in this book use these letters so they can sound out each letter and blend them together to read the words.

Ⓦ Ask the children to find and point to the first word on the first page, then look at the picture on pages 4 and 5 and find the same word written on the picture (*Tom*). Remind them that names and sentences begin with capital letters. Ask them to point to the matching lower case letter in the box on the back cover and say the letter sound.

Strategy check

Look at the book cover together. Sound out and blend the words in the title. Remind the children to sound out and blend any words in the story that they do not recognise.

Independent reading

Ⓦ Encourage each of the children to read the whole book at his or her own pace, sounding out and blending words they do not recognise.

● Praise the children for sounding out and blending sounds to read words they do not recognise and for recognising familiar words.

Assessment Observe the children to check that they can:

▪ *(R, AF1)* point at the text, moving along the line from left to right

▪ *(R, AF1)* confidently give the sound for all the focus letter patterns, including the capital letters *T, P, S*

▪ *(R, AF1)* successfully blend the three sounds for *got* together and recognise it as the word *got*

▪ *(R, AF1)* recognise the repeated words (*pat* and *tap*) on pages 4 and 6.

Emphasise and model these skills for any child who needs help.

Returning to the text

Ask the children to:

Ⓒ *(Clarifying)* Find the picture of a cap. Find a picture of something else that rhymes with *cap* (*tap*).

(W) Think of other words that rhyme with *cap* (*gap, lap, nap, yap, chap, clap, flap*).

(W) Segment *cap* into its separate sounds, ready for writing. Have a go at writing *cap* on a board. Blend the sounds together again.

(W) *Change one letter*

Ask the children to change one letter of *cap* to write *map, then tap,* and *tag.*

(W) Find the word *pot* in the text. Think of other words that rhyme with *pot* (*dot, hot, got, jot, lot, not, rot*).

(W) Close the book and segment *pot* into its separate sounds, ready for writing. Have a go at writing *pot* on a board. Blend the sounds together again. Find it in the book to check.

(W) *Change one letter*

Ask the children to change one letter of *pot* to write *got*, then *cot*, then *cop*.

Assessment Observe the children to check that they can:

▪ *(R, AF1)* generate words that rhyme

▪ *(R, AF1)* segment *cap* and *pot* into their separate sounds, remembering the letters which represent those sounds.

Model the appropriate responses for children who need help. Follow this up with further practice using the Blending Activity, Letter Pattern Activity and Segmenting Activity for *Sam's Pot* on the *eSongb*irds CD-ROM, as well as additional practice reading *Sam's Pot* using the Talking Story version.

Where next?

Further phonic practice

(W) Find the picture of the cat. Find a picture of something else which rhymes with *cat* (*mat*). Think of other words that end with the sound *t* (*bat, sat, pot, cot, not*).

(W) Segment *mat* into its separate sounds, ready for writing. Write *mat* on a board, saying each sound in isolation as you write it. Then blend the sounds together while pointing at each sound. Find it in the book to check.

Extension phonic work

(W) Ask the children to help write and illustrate a Rhyme Book. Develop the sentence *Tom got a pot* in a shared writing session. Finish these sentences with a rhyming word, e.g. *Pat got a …* (*cat, mat*), *Dot got a …* (*pot, cot*).

Bob Bug

Focus phonics					
r	rug rat	**i**	is his big fit it lid sip	**g**	bug big rug hug
l	lid	**u**	bug mum cup rug hug	**p**	cup sip
d	dad lid bad	**s**	is has his sip	**a**	has dad bad rat
b	bob bug big bad	**m**	mum	**o**	Bob cot
f	fit	**c**	cup cot		
h	has his hug	**t**	fit it cot rat		

C = Language comprehension   *R, AF* = QCA reading assessment focus

W = Word recognition   *W, AF* = QCA writing assessment focus

Introducing the phonics

W Make letter cards by writing the focus letters on individual pieces of card. Stress the correct letter formation as you do so and encourage the children to sky-write the letters.

W *Quick sounds*
Ask the children to say the sound usually made by each letter as you point to it. Vary the order.

W *Blending sounds*
Draw three boxes in a row, as a phoneme frame, on a board. Display the letter cards (or magnetic letters) around it. Pick three cards and place them, one in each box, to make a word *(bug, hug, rug, lid, hip, fit)*. Tell the children that each of these letters makes one sound in a word. Ask the children to say the sound of each letter as you point to it then blend the letters together to read the word.

Group or guided reading

Before reading

W Ask the children to tell you the sound usually made by each letter in the box on the back cover of their books.

W Tell the children that the words in this book use these letters so they can sound out each letter and blend them together to read the words.

W Look carefully at the *b* and *d*. Ask the children to make a bed shape by putting their fists together and sticking their thumbs upwards. Point out that the left hand makes the beginning sound of *bed*, *b*, and the right hand makes the end sound, *d*.

Strategy check

Look again at the letters in the box on the back of the book. Ask the children to say each letter sound. Tell the children to look out for them as they read. Remind them to sound out and blend words they do not recognise.

Independent reading

W Encourage each of the children to read the whole book at his or her own pace, sounding out and blending words they do not recognise. Listen in to each child reading and provide lots of praise and support.

● Praise children for matching one spoken word to one written word.

● Praise them for sounding out and blending sounds to read words they do not recognise, and for recognising familiar words.

Assessment Observe the children to check that they can:

▪ *(R, AF1)* match one spoken word to one written word

▪ *(R, AF1)* confidently give the sound for all the focus letters

▪ *(R, AF1)* successfully blend the three sounds for *mum* together and recognise it as the word *mum*

▪ *(R, AF1)* correctly sound out the *b* and *d* in *bad* on page 7, without confusion.

Emphasise and model these skills for any child who needs help.

Returning to the text

Ask the children to:

C *(Questioning, Clarifying)* Explain what frightened Bob Bug. (A shadow in the shape of a rat.) Explain what made him feel better. (A hug.)

W Make a *b* with their left fist. Find a word in the text beginning with the sound *b* *(bug, big, bad)*, sound out all the letters in the word and then blend them together to read the word.

Ⓦ Find something else in the pictures that begins with the sound *b (bus, ball, bib)*.

Ⓦ Segment *bib* into its separate sounds, ready for writing and write it on a board. Blend the sounds together again to read the word.

Ⓦ Make a *d* with their right fist. Find a word in the text ending with the sound *d*, sound out all the letters in the word and then blend them together to read the word *(dad, lid, bad)*.

Ⓦ Close the book. Segment *bad* into its separate sounds ready for writing and write it on a whiteboard. Blend the sounds together again to read the word. Find it in the book to check.

Assessment Observe the children to check that they can:

◼ *(R, AF2)* follow the meaning of the text recalling significant events

◼ *(R, AF1)* remember the sound and correct orientation of the letters *b* and *d*

◼ *(R, AF1)* segment *bib* and *bad* into their separate sounds, remembering the letters which represent those sounds.

Model the appropriate responses for children who need help. Follow this up with further practice using the Blending Activity, Letter Pattern Activity and Segmenting Activity for *Bob Bug* on the *eSongbirds* CD-ROM, as well as additional practice reading *Bob Bug* using the Talking Story version.

Where next?

Further phonic practice

Ⓦ Ask the children to segment *big* into its separate sounds, ready for writing. Write *big* on a board, saying each sound in isolation as you write it. Then blend the sounds together while pointing at each sound. Find it in the book to check.

Ⓦ Ask the children to segment *bug* into its separate sounds and write it on a board.

Ⓦ *Change one letter*
Ask the children to change one letter of *bug* to write *rug*, then *hug*, then *hut*, then *hum*.

Extension phonic work

Ⓒ *(Clarifying)* Ask the children to draw characters from the story from their own families. Add speech bubbles calling out names *(Mum! Dad! Bob Bug!)*. Explain that the exclamation mark shows that the characters are calling.

Dig, Dig, Dig!

Focus phonics					
r	rag	*i*	dig Tim his lid big tin in it	*p*	up
l	lot lid lots	*u*	fun dug up mud bus bugs	*a*	had rag and
d	dog dig had dug mud lid and	*s*	his bus lots bugs	*o*	dog lot lots
b	bus big bugs	*m*	Tim mud	*n*	fun tin in and
f	fun	*t*	Tim lot tin it lots		
h	his had	*g*	dig dog dug rag big bugs		

C = Language comprehension   *R, AF* = QCA reading assessment focus

W = Word recognition   *W, AF* = QCA writing assessment focus

Introducing the phonics

W *Robot Talk*

Use a puppet or a robot made out of junk materials to say words in a special robotic way. Tell the children the robot says all the sounds in words separately and they have to blend the sounds together to tell you what the robot is saying. Make the robot say the focus phonics words (e.g. *d – o – g, b – u – s, l – i – d*). Display objects or pictures to help the children if you have them.

W *Spot the vowel sound*

Display letter cards of the focus vowel sounds, *a, i, o, u*. Tell the children that you are going to say some words that have these letters in the middle. Say a word containing one of these vowels *(cat, bib, mop, rug)*. Ask the children to show you the letter used to make this sound using the letter cards, letter fans or on a board.

W Introduce the plural *s* and practise blending sounds. Draw four boxes in a row, as a phoneme frame, on a board. Display the focus letter cards (or magnetic letters) around it. Write the numeral *2* in front of the frame then pick three cards and place them, one in each of the first boxes *(cat, mat, mop, pot, rug, lid)*. Ask the children to say the sound of each letter as you point to it, then blend the letters together to read the word. Read the whole phrase, e.g. *2 cat*. Ask the children what is wrong. Ask someone to come and put the correct letter in the end sound box to make the word say, e.g. *cats*.

Group or guided reading

Before reading

Ⓦ Ask the children to tell you the sound usually made by each letter in the box on the back cover of their books.

Ⓦ Tell the children that most of the words in this book use these letters so they can sound out each letter and blend them together to read the words.

Ⓦ Explain that it is important when blending the sounds in a word together to check to see if it sounds like a real word. Point out that in *of*, the *f* makes an unusual *v* sound.

Strategy check

Say the letter sounds in the box on the back of the book together. Ask children to say each letter sound. Tell the children to look out for them as they read. Remind them to sound out and blend words they do not recognise.

Independent reading

Ⓦ Encourage each of the children to read the whole book at his or her own pace, sounding out and blending words they do not recognise. Listen in to each child reading and provide lots of praise and support.

● Praise the children for sounding out and blending sounds to read words they do not recognise and for recognising familiar words.

Assessment Observe the children to check that they can:

■ *(R, AF1)* match one spoken word to one written word

■ *(R, AF1)* confidently give the sound for all the focus letter patterns

■ *(R, AF1)* successfully blend the sounds for *mud* together and recognise it as the word *mud*

■ *(R, AF1)* correctly sound out the letters in *bugs* on page 8 and blend all four together successfully.

Emphasise and model these skills for any child who needs help.

Returning to the text

Ask the children to:

C *(Questioning, Summarising)* Recall what the dog dug up in order.

C *(Summarising)* Write the things dug up in order on a board *(mud, rag, bus, lid, tin, bugs)*. (Remind the children to segment the things into separate sounds, write the sounds down then blend them together to read what they have written. Then look in the book and check.)

W Find words in the text with *u* as the middle vowel sound. Sound out all the letters in the words and then blend them together to read the words *(fun, dug, mud, bus)*.

Assessment Observe the children to check that they can:

▪ *(R, AF1)* recognise given letter shapes and say the sound for each

▪ *(R, AF1)* follow the meaning of the text recalling significant events in the correct sequence

▪ *(W, AF8)* segment CVC words into their separate sounds for writing, remembering the letters which represent those sounds.

Model the appropriate responses for children who need help. Follow this up with further practice using the Blending Activity, Letter Pattern Activity and Segmenting Activity for *Dig, Dig, Dig!* on the *eSongbirds* CD-ROM, as well as additional practice reading *Dig, Dig, Dig!* using the Talking Story version.

Where next?

Further phonic practice

W Ask the children to find words in the text with *i* as the middle vowel sound *(dig, Tim, his, lid, big, tin)*. Sound out all the letters in the words and then blend them together to read the words. Think of other words containing this sound *(wig, jig, him, hid, kid, bin, din, fin)*.

Extension phonic work

W Ask the children to write and illustrate a number frieze. Use cvc words which become plural by adding *s (cat, rat, bat, hat, pot, top, mop, tap, cap, rug, mug, bug, can, pan, fan, pin, tin, bin, dog)*.

Zak and the Vet

Focus phonics					
v	van vet	**r**	ran red	**m**	him
w	went wag	**d**	did and red had bad	**c**	cut
y	yes	**b**	bad jab	**t**	sit not went vet cut get
z	Zak	**f**	fog	**g**	fog get wag
j	Jen jab	**h**	hit him had	**a**	Zak ran and van had bad jab wag
n	not ran in Jen and van went	**i**	sit did in hit him	**o**	not fog
k	Zak	**u**	cut		
e	red Jen went vet get yes	**s**	sit yes		

C = Language comprehension   *R, AF* = QCA reading assessment focus

W = Word recognition   *W, AF* = QCA writing assessment focus

Introducing the phonics

W Make letter cards by writing the focus letters on individual pieces of card. Stress the correct letter formation as you do so and encourage the children to sky-write the letters.

W *Quick sounds*
Ask the children to say the sound usually made by each letter as you point to it. Vary the order.

W Ask the children to tell you which letters both make the sound *c* (as in *cat*). Make a collection of words containing the *c* sound. Underline the letters which makes the *c* sound (e.g. *c̲at, c̲up, c̲an, c̲ub, k̲it, k̲id, yu̲k*).

W *Segmenting Sounds.*
Draw three boxes in a row, as a phoneme frame, on a board. Display the letter cards around it. Name a word for an animal using the focus letters *(e.g. cat, dog, hen, kid, bat, yak, rat)*. Ask the children to segment the word into all its sounds and then place the three cards that make those sounds, one

in each box, to write the word. Ask all the children to say the sound of each letter as you point to it then blend the letters together to read the word.

Group or guided reading

Before reading

(W) Ask the children to tell you the sound usually made by each letter in the box on the back cover of their books. Tell the children that most of the words in this book use these letters so they can sound out each letter and blend them together to read the words.

(W) Explain that it is important when blending the sounds in a word together to check to see if it sounds like a real word as some words are less regular. Introduce the children to the context words (see page 5, or the inside back cover of *Zak and the Vet*) by writing them on a board. Read these words and point out the letters that make the usual sound in each word *(e.g. h in he)*.

(C) *(Clarifying)* Look at the cover and discuss where the story is set and what a vet does. Introduce the word *jab* to describe an injection.

Strategy check

Check that the children recognise the focus phonics listed on the back cover. Use the title on the cover to practise segmenting and blending sounds. Remind the children to do this if they meet a word they do not know.

Independent reading

(W) Encourage each of the children to read the whole book at his or her own pace, sounding out and blending words they do not recognise. Listen in to each child reading and provide lots of praise and support.

● Praise the children for sounding out and blending sounds to read words they do not recognise and for recognising familiar words.

Assessment Observe the children to check that they can:

▨ *(R, AF1)* match one spoken word to one written word

▨ *(R, AF1)* confidently give the sounds for the focus letters

▨ *(R, AF1)* successfully blend the three sounds of *vet* together and recognise it as the word *vet*.

Emphasise and model these skills for any child who needs help.

Returning to the text

Ask the children to:

(W) Find words in the text beginning with the sound *v*. Sound out all the letters in the words, then blend them together to read them *(vet, van)*.

(W) Shut the book and segment *vet* into its separate sounds ready for writing, and write the word on a board. Blend the sounds together again. Find it in the book to check.

(W) *Change One Letter*
Change one letter of *vet to* write *wet,* then *web,* then *wed,* then *bed,* then *bad,* then *bid,* then *bud.*

(C) *(Summarising)* Ask the children to explain why Zak was in the road.

(C) *(Imagining)* Ask them to say what they would do to keep Zak safe, if Zak were their dog.

Assessment   Observe the children to check that they can:

■ *(R, AF2)* follow the meaning of the text, and say what they think should happen next

■ *(R, AF1)* remember the letter that makes the sound *v*

■ *(R, AF1)* confidently use sounding and blending to tackle words out of context.

Model the appropriate responses for children who need help. Follow this up with further practice using the Blending Activity, Letter Pattern Activity and Segmenting Activity for *Zak and the Vet* on the *eSongbirds* CD-ROM, as well as additional practice reading *Zak and the Vet* using the Talking Story version.

Where next?

Further phonic practice

(W) Ask the children to find a word in the book where the *c* sound is represented by the letter *k (Zak)*. Close the book. Segment the word into its separate sounds and write it on a board, remembering the capital letter. Blend the sounds together.

Extension phonic work

(C) *(Imagining)* Ask the children to design and make a poster showing how to cross a road safely.

Mum Bug's Bag

Focus phonics							
w	wet	*d*	red and	*c*	can
y	yuk	*b*	Bug bag bun big	*t*	fit pot get gets wet
z	zip	*f*	fit fan	*g*	Bug bag get gets big
j	jam	*h*	has	*p*	zip pen pot
n	can pen in fan and bun	*i*	zip fit in big	*a*	has fan bag can and jam
k	yuk	*u*	Mum Bug bun yuk	*o*	pot
e	red pen gets wet	*s*	has gets		
r	red	*m*	Mum jam		

C = Language comprehension   *R, AF* = QCA reading assessment focus

W = Word recognition   *W, AF* = QCA writing assessment focus

Introducing the phonics

W *Robot talk*

Place objects (or pictures of objects) that are written with the focus letters in a bag: *pen, cat, jug, net, can, bed, kid, wig, zip, yak, peg, cup, fan.* Use a puppet to name the things in the bag in a special robotic way. Tell the children the puppet says all the sounds in words separately and they have to blend the sounds together to tell you what the puppet is saying. Ask the children to take turns to be the puppet.

W *Segmenting sounds*

Draw three boxes in a row, as a phoneme frame, on a board. Display the letter cards (or magnetic letters) around it. Ask the children to pick one of the objects from the bag, segment the word into all its sounds and then place the three cards that make those sounds, one in each box, to write the word. Ask all the children to say the sound of each letter as you point to it, then blend the letters together to read the word. Point out words where the *c* sound is written with a letter *c* (*cat, cup, can*) and words where the *c* sound is written with a letter *k* (*kid, yak*).

Group or guided reading

Before reading

W Ask the children to tell you the sound usually made by each letter in the box on the back cover of their books. Ask them: *Which letters both make the sound c (as in cat)*? Tell the children that most of the words in this book use these letters so they can sound out each letter and blend them together to read the words. Explain that it is important when blending the sounds in a word together to check to see if it sounds like a real word as some words are less regular.

W Introduce the children to the context words (see page 5, or the inside back cover of *Mum Bug's Bag*) by writing them on a board. Read these words and point out the letters that make the usual sound in each word (e.g. the *h* in *her*). This will help the children to remember these words.

Strategy check

Ask the children to show you how they would say the sounds and then blend the letters in each word in the title on the cover. Remind them to do this when they meet a new word in the story.

Independent reading

W Encourage each of the children to read the whole book at his or her own pace, sounding out and blending words they do not recognise. Listen in to each child reading and provide lots of praise and support.

● Praise the children for sounding out and blending sounds to read words they do not recognise.

● Praise them for matching one spoken word to one written word.

Assessment Observe the children to check that they can:

■ *(R, AF1)* confidently give the sound for all the focus letters

■ *(R, AF1)* successfully blend all the sounds for the word *red* together and recognise it as the word *red*

■ *(R, AF1)* match one spoken word to one written word.

Emphasise and model these skills for any child who needs help.

Returning to the text

Ask the children to:

(C) *(Questioning, Summarising)* Recall what Mum had in her bag in order (*pen, fan, bun, jam*).

(W) Write the things in Mum's bag on the board. (Remind the children to segment the words into separate sounds, write the sounds down then blend them together to read what they have written.

(W) *Change One Letter*
Change one letter of *jam* to write *jab*, then *job*, then *jot*, then *jet*, then *net*, then *nut*, then *but*, then *bit*.

Assessment Observe the children to check that they can:

■ *(R, AF2)* follow the meaning of the text, recalling events in the correct sequence

■ *(R, AF1)* segment CVC words into their separate sounds, remembering the letters which represent those sounds

■ *(W, AF8)* use phonic knowledge to write simple regular words.

Model the appropriate responses for children who need help. Follow this up with further practice using the Blending Activity, Letter Pattern Activity and Segmenting Activity for *Mum Bug's Bag* on the *eSongbirds* CD-ROM, as well as additional practice reading *Mum Bug's Bag* using the Talking Story version.

Where next?

Further phonic practice

(W) Ask the children to find a picture in this book of something that rhymes with *can (pan)*. Segment *pan* into its separate sounds and write it on a board. Blend the sounds together again to read the word. Change one letter to make *pen*. Look in the book and check.

(W) Ask the children to look in the book and find a picture of something that rhymes with *bun (sun)*. Segment *sun* into its separate sounds and write it on a board. Blend the sounds together again to read the word. Change one letter to make it say *fun*, then *fin*.

Extension phonic work

(C) *(Imagining)* Ask the children to write and illustrate a bag story. Use the following sentence structure: *I can fit a _ _ _ in my bag.*

Oxford Reading Tree resources at this level

There is a range of material available at a similar level to these stories which can be used for consolidation or extension.

Stage 1+

Teacher support
For developing phonics
- Rhyme and Analogy First Story Rhymes
- Rhyme and Analogy First Story Rhymes Tapes
- Alphabet Frieze
- Tabletop Alphabet Mats,
- Alphabet Photocopy Masters
- Card Games

Further reading
- ORT First Phonics
- ORT Biff, Chip and Kipper Stories
- ORT Floppy's Phonics
- Snapdragons Stories
- Glow-worms Poetry
- Fireflies and More Fireflies Non-Fiction

Electronic
- First Phonics Talking Stories and activities
- First Story Rhymes
- Rhyme and Analogy Activity Software
- Talking Stories
- eSongbirds CD-ROM
- Clip Art
- Storytapes
- Floppy and Friends CD-ROM
- ORT Online www.OxfordReadingTree.com
- MagicPage CD-ROM

OXFORD
UNIVERSITY PRESS

Great Clarendon Street, Oxford OX2 6DP

Oxford University Press is a department of the University of Oxford.
It furthers the University's objective of excellence in research, scholarship, and education by publishing worldwide in

Oxford New York

Auckland Cape Town Dar es Salaam Hong Kong Karachi
Kuala Lumpur Madrid Melbourne Mexico City Nairobi
New Delhi Shanghai Taipei Toronto

With offices in
Argentina Austria Brazil Chile Czech Republic France Greece
Guatemala Hungary Italy Japan Poland Portugal Singapore
South Korea Switzerland Thailand Turkey Ukraine Vietnam

Oxford is a registered trade mark of Oxford University Press
in the UK and in certain other countries

First published 2008

British Library Cataloguing in Publication Data

Data available

Cover illustration by Pauline Siewert

ISBN: 978-019-846660-4

10 9 8 7 6 5 4 3

Printed in China by Imago

Paper used in the production of this book is a natural, recyclable product made from wood grown in sustainable forests. The manufacturing process conforms to the environmental regulations of the country of origin